# Legends of Loch Ness

# Legends of Loch Ness

Thomas Shelton

# CONTENTS

# Introduction to Loch Ness and Its Mystique

## Overview of Loch Ness

Loch Ness, a large freshwater lake located in the Scottish Highlands, is renowned for its stunning natural beauty and its enigmatic reputation as the home of the elusive Loch Ness Monster. Stretching approximately 23 miles in length and reaching depths of over 700 feet, Loch Ness is not only one of the largest bodies of water in Scotland but also one of the most fascinating. The loch's deep, dark waters and surrounding rugged landscapes create an atmosphere ripe for legends and folklore, drawing tourists and cryptozoology enthusiasts alike to explore its mysteries.

The lore surrounding the Loch Ness Monster dates back centuries, with historical accounts of sightings and encounters that have captivated the imagination of many. The earliest references can be traced to the 6th century, when St. Columba reportedly encountered a beast in the loch, which was believed to be a dragon-like creature. Over the years, numerous reports have emerged, ranging from vague glimpses of a large shape moving beneath the water to detailed descriptions of a long-necked creature. These accounts have fueled the legend of Nessie, making it a central figure in Scottish folklore.

In the realm of cryptozoology, Loch Ness has become a focal point for those searching for evidence of the existence of unknown creatures. Various expeditions and investigations have taken place over the years, employing a range of technologies from sonar mapping to underwater cameras in hopes of capturing definitive proof of the monster. Despite the fervent enthusiasm and numerous claims, scientific investigations have yet to yield conclusive evidence supporting the creature's existence. Nonetheless, the ongoing search continues to spark debates and discussions within the community, making Loch Ness a hotspot for cryptozoological inquiry.

The Loch Ness Monster's influence extends beyond folklore and scientific investigation; it has permeated popular culture in profound ways. From documentaries and television series to movies and literature, Nessie has become an iconic symbol of mystery and intrigue. This cultural representation often shapes public perception, with artistic interpretations ranging from whimsical to fearsome. As such, the Loch Ness Monster has become a part of Scotland's identity, attracting tourists eager to explore the landscape that inspired countless stories and artistic works.

Tourism plays a significant role in the economy surrounding Loch Ness, with various attractions dedicated to the monster phenomenon. Visitors flock to the area for boat tours, exhibitions, and themed events that celebrate the legend of Nessie. However, this influx of tourism also raises questions about the environmental impact on the loch and its ecosystem. The delicate balance between conservation and the desire to explore and enjoy the natural beauty of Loch Ness is a concern for both locals and environmentalists. Ultimately, the legend of the Loch Ness Monster continues to enchant and inspire, reflecting a deep-seated psychological fascination with the unknown and the enduring allure of cryptids.

## The Legend of the Loch Ness Monster

The legend of the Loch Ness Monster, affectionately known as Nessie, has captured the imagination of people around the world for nearly a century. This enigmatic creature is said to inhabit Loch Ness, a large freshwater lake in the Scottish Highlands, and is often described as a large, long-necked being resembling a plesiosaur. The first modern sighting can be traced back to 1933 when a couple claimed to have seen a large creature moving in the water, leading to an explosion of interest and subsequent reports of sightings. This event marked the beginning of a phenomenon that would intertwine local folklore, scientific curiosity, and popular culture.

Over the decades, numerous accounts of alleged encounters with Nessie have emerged, contributing to the rich tapestry of Loch Ness lore. From grainy photographs and sonar readings to eyewitness testimonies, these historical accounts have fueled both skepticism and belief. Notably, the 1934 surgeon's photograph, which purportedly showed Nessie's head and neck, became one of the most famous images in cryptozoology, although it was later revealed to be a hoax. Despite the debunking of some evidence, the legend persists, with many visitors to Loch Ness claiming to have witnessed the creature themselves.

The search for the Loch Ness Monster has sparked a variety of scientific investigations, ranging from sonar explorations to environmental studies aimed at understanding the lake's ecology. Researchers have employed advanced technology in their quests, including underwater cameras and drones, seeking concrete evidence of Nessie's existence. While the scientific community remains largely skeptical, these efforts have provided valuable insights into the biodiversity of Loch Ness and its surroundings, highlighting the importance of conservation and the environmental impact of tourism on this iconic location.

Nessie has also become an enduring symbol in popular culture, inspiring books, films, and various media representations. The creature has appeared in everything from children's cartoons to serious documentaries, each interpretation shaping public perception of Loch Ness and its mythical inhabitant. This cultural phenomenon has further enhanced the allure of Loch Ness as a tourist destination, with visitors flocking to the area in hopes of catching a glimpse of the elusive beast or purchasing memorabilia that celebrates the legend.

The psychology of belief in cryptids like the Loch Ness Monster plays a significant role in the ongoing fascination with Nessie. Cultural narratives, personal experiences, and the human tendency to find patterns in the unknown contribute to the persistence of the legend. For many, the possibility of a creature lurking beneath the water represents the intersection of myth and reality, offering a sense of wonder and adventure. As long as stories of the Loch Ness Monster continue to be told, the legend will remain an integral part of Scottish folklore, inviting both skepticism and belief in equal measure.

# 2

# Historical Accounts of Loch Ness Monster Sightings

## Early Sightings and Accounts

The early sightings and accounts of the Loch Ness Monster form an essential foundation for understanding the legend that has captivated imaginations for centuries. Historical records indicate that the Loch Ness area has long been steeped in tales of mysterious creatures lurking beneath the water's surface. The first known mention of a monster in Loch Ness dates back to the 6th century, when the Irish monk St. Columba reportedly encountered a beast while on a pilgrimage. This account, though anecdotal, set the stage for a tradition of monster sightings that would evolve and grow over the centuries.

As time progressed, the folklore surrounding Loch Ness began to intertwine with the lives of local inhabitants. In the early 20th century, the first modern sightings were reported, notably in 1933, when a couple claimed to have seen an enormous creature crossing the road near the loch. This incident sparked widespread media coverage, leading to a surge of interest in the monster. Newspapers across Scotland and beyond published sensational stories, transforming the Loch Ness Monster into a cultural phenomenon. These early sightings not only fueled public fascination but also laid the groundwork for subsequent investigations and searches.

Throughout the years, numerous accounts have emerged, each adding layers to the mythos of the Loch Ness Monster. Witness testimonies describe everything from large, undulating shapes to a creature resembling a prehistoric dinosaur. The diversity of these descriptions reflects not only the varying perspectives of those who claim to have seen the creature but also the psychological factors at play in belief systems surrounding cryptids. This phenomenon highlights how local folklore can shape perceptions, leading individuals to interpret ambiguous stimuli in ways that align with cultural narratives.

Scientific investigations into the Loch Ness Monster have sought to validate or debunk these early accounts. Various expeditions have employed sonar technology and underwater photography in attempts to capture definitive evidence of the creature. However, despite extensive research, conclusive proof remains elusive. This ongoing search embodies the spirit of cryptozoology, where enthusiasts balance skepticism with a willingness to explore the unknown. The blending of folklore, personal testimonies, and scientific inquiry creates a rich tapestry of narratives that keep the legend alive.

The impact of these early sightings reverberates through popular culture, tourism, and artistic representations. From documentaries to feature films, the Loch Ness Monster has been portrayed in countless ways, often reinforcing the mystique surrounding the loch. Local businesses have capitalized on this fascination, offering monster-themed attractions and tours that draw visitors from around the globe. As these accounts continue to inspire both curiosity and skepticism, they form a crucial part of the ongoing dialogue about the Loch Ness Monster, ensuring that its legacy remains vibrant in the collective imagination.

## The Surge of Interest in the 20th Century

The 20th century marked a significant turning point in the cultural narrative surrounding the Loch Ness Monster, igniting a surge of interest that would intertwine folklore, scientific inquiry, and popular culture. The iconic image of the monster, often referred to as "Nessie," began to capture the imagination of people far beyond Scotland's borders. This period saw a notable increase in reported sightings, particularly after the infamous photograph known as the "Surgeon's Photograph" surfaced in 1934. Although later revealed as a hoax, this image solidified Nessie's place in popular culture and sparked a wave of curiosity and exploration into the depths of Loch Ness.

As the 20th century progressed, the fascination with the Loch Ness Monster expanded into various forms of media, including literature, film, and television. Documentaries and sensationalist news reports proliferated, each contributing to the mystique surrounding the creature. These portrayals often blended historical accounts with speculative narratives, shaping public perception and encouraging further exploration. The Loch Ness Monster became not only a subject of scientific investigation but also a perennial topic for entertainment, captivating audiences with stories of mysterious sightings and daring expeditions to uncover the truth.

The rise of cryptozoology as a field in the mid-20th century fueled the quest for Nessie, attracting enthusiasts and researchers dedicated to proving the existence of unknown creatures. This burgeoning discipline sought to apply scientific methods to folklore, promoting rigorous investigations while simultaneously legitimizing the stories passed down through generations. Prominent figures in the field, such as Dr. Neil Gemmell, have conducted genetic studies of Loch Ness water samples, hoping to find tangible evidence of the monster's existence. This blend of folklore and science has created a unique dialogue, inviting both skeptics and believers to engage in discussions about the nature of belief and the evidence that shapes it.

Tourism also played a pivotal role in the surge of interest during this century. The Loch Ness Monster became a cornerstone of Scotland's tourism industry, with countless visitors flocking to the loch to catch a glimpse of the enigmatic creature. Tourist attractions, including boat tours and exhibitions dedicated to Nessie, emerged, promoting local folklore while simultaneously addressing environmental concerns. The impact of increased tourism on Loch Ness's ecosystem has raised important questions about conservation and the balance between preserving natural habitats and catering to the demands of curious travelers.

The 20th century's fascination with the Loch Ness Monster continues to resonate in contemporary society, reflecting broader themes of mystery, belief, and the human desire to uncover the unknown. The legends surrounding Nessie serve as a testament to the power of storytelling and the enduring allure of cryptids in popular culture. As new technologies and methodologies evolve, the quest for the Loch Ness Monster remains a captivating narrative, drawing in countless enthusiasts eager to connect with the rich tapestry of folklore and history that Loch Ness embodies.

## Notable Eyewitness Testimonies

Eyewitness testimonies play a crucial role in the lore surrounding the Loch Ness Monster, adding a layer of human experience to the cryptozoological narrative. From the earliest accounts to modern sightings, these testimonies reflect a diverse range of perspectives, each contributing to the enduring mystery of Loch Ness. Notably, the most famous sighting, often referred to as the "surgeon's photograph" taken in 1934, has become an iconic representation of the creature. Although later deemed a hoax, this image galvanized public interest and inspired countless individuals to seek out their own encounters with what they believed to be the elusive monster.

In the decades since, many have reported sightings of strange creatures in the loch, each story adding to the tapestry of local folklore. For instance, in the 1960s, a group of tourists claimed to have seen a large, dark shape moving beneath the water, only to be met with skepticism by some and intrigue by others. These accounts, whether substantiated or not, reveal the deep psychological and cultural impact that the Loch Ness Monster has on those who visit the area. The emotional weight of these experiences often transcends mere observation, becoming woven into the personal narratives of the witnesses.

The testimonies of local residents also provide a fascinating insight into the lore of Loch Ness. Generations of families have shared stories of mysterious disturbances on the loch, often passed down through oral tradition. These accounts frequently emphasize the connection between the landscape and the supernatural, highlighting how the natural beauty of Loch Ness becomes a backdrop for reports of otherworldly encounters. For locals, the monster is not just a tourist attraction but a symbol of their heritage and a testament to the rich tapestry of myths that define their community.

Scientific investigations into these testimonies have sought to validate or refute the claims made by witnesses. Researchers have employed various methodologies, such as sonar explorations and underwater photography, to uncover the truth behind the legends. While some scientific efforts have produced interesting findings, none have conclusively proven the existence of a large creature in the loch. This ongoing quest for evidence only fuels the intrigue surrounding eyewitness accounts, as enthusiasts continue to grapple with the intersection of belief and skepticism in the search for the Loch Ness Monster.

The impact of eyewitness testimonies extends beyond the realm of cryptozoology, influencing popular culture in significant ways. Films, documentaries, and literature have all been inspired by these accounts, shaping the public's perception of the Loch Ness Monster. As stories of sightings circulate in the media, they often take on a life of their own, contributing to the mythos surrounding the creature. This dynamic interplay between personal experiences and cultural representation underscores the enduring fascination with the Loch Ness Monster, ensuring that it remains a captivating subject for both tourists and cryptozoology enthusiasts alike.

# 3

# Cryptozoology and the Search for Nessie

## Definition and Scope of Cryptozoology

Cryptozoology is a fascinating field that straddles the line between science and folklore, dedicated to the study of creatures whose existence has not been substantiated by mainstream science. It encompasses a wide range of entities, from legendary beasts like the Loch Ness Monster to creatures mentioned in local myths across the globe. The term itself, derived from the Greek words "kryptos" meaning hidden, and "zoology," refers to the investigation of animals that are rumored to exist but have not been formally recognized by zoological standards. This subfield offers a unique lens through which to explore cultural beliefs, historical narratives, and the human tendency to seek out the unknown.

The scope of cryptozoology is broad, as it not only includes the investigation of specific creatures but also the cultural, historical, and psychological contexts surrounding them. In the case of the Loch Ness Monster, enthusiasts delve into a myriad of historical accounts and sightings that contribute to the ongoing intrigue surrounding this elusive creature. Sightings date back to ancient times, with numerous reports surfacing over the decades, each adding layers to the legend. Cryptozoologists examine these accounts critically, assessing the reliability of witnesses and the context in which these sightings occurred. Such investigations contribute to a larger conversation about the intersection of mythology and reality.

Additionally, cryptozoology often intersects with scientific inquiry, as researchers employ various methodologies to gather evidence. This may include sonar mapping of Loch Ness, analysis of water samples, and even the examination of photographic evidence. Despite the skepticism that often surrounds the field, these scientific investigations aim to uncover tangible proof of cryptids, which can sometimes yield surprising results. Enthusiasts are drawn to the thrill of potential discovery, and the ongoing search for the Loch Ness Monster serves as a case study in the complex relationship between belief and evidence.

The cultural significance of the Loch Ness Monster cannot be overstated, as it has permeated popular culture in various forms, from literature to film and television. Representations of the creature often reflect societal beliefs and fears, serving as a canvas for artistic expression. Documentaries and television series have captivated audiences, blending fact and fiction to create a narrative that keeps the legend alive. These portrayals not only entertain but also inform public perception and influence tourism, with countless visitors flocking to Loch Ness in search of both the monster and the folklore that surrounds it.

Ultimately, the psychology of belief in cryptids like the Loch Ness Monster plays a crucial role in the field of cryptozoology. The allure of the unknown and the possibility of discovering a living relic from prehistoric times resonate deeply with human curiosity. Tourists and enthusiasts alike find themselves drawn to the mystery, engaging with local folklore and legends that enrich their experience of Loch Ness. This engagement fosters a deeper connection to the environment and an appreciation for the stories that shape our understanding of the natural world, revealing that cryptozoology is not merely about the search for hidden creatures but also about exploring the human experience itself.

## Methods of Investigation

Methods of investigation into the Loch Ness Monster encompass a blend of traditional folklore analysis, scientific inquiry, and modern technological advancements. Cryptozoologists, historians, and enthusiasts alike employ a variety of strategies to sift through the rich tapestry of accounts surrounding this enigmatic creature. One prominent method involves the examination of historical documents and eyewitness testimonies, allowing researchers to track the evolution of the monster's legend. By analyzing newspaper clippings, journals, and local folklore, investigators can discern patterns in sightings and understand how cultural context shapes the narrative surrounding the Loch Ness Monster.

In addition to historical analysis, scientific investigations play a crucial role in the search for evidence of the creature's existence. Researchers have employed sonar technology to scan the depths of Loch Ness, aiming to capture any unusual aquatic life forms. These sonar expeditions have produced intriguing results over the years, including unidentified large objects that have sparked further interest and speculation. Moreover, water sampling has been conducted to analyze biological materials, searching for DNA that could potentially confirm the presence of unknown species. Such scientific methodologies not only aim to uncover tangible evidence but also contribute to the broader discourse on biodiversity in the loch.

Another essential method of investigation is the use of modern technology, including underwater drones and remote sensing equipment. These tools allow researchers to explore areas of Loch Ness that are difficult to access, providing a new perspective on the loch's depths. The incorporation of high-resolution cameras and thermal imaging has enabled investigators to capture clearer visuals of the underwater environment, offering insights into the habitat that may sustain elusive creatures. This technological approach complements traditional methods, creating a multifaceted investigation that appeals to both scientific rigor and the allure of the unknown.

Field studies and community engagement also play a significant role in the investigation of the Loch Ness Monster. Researchers often collaborate with local residents and tourists, gathering anecdotal evidence and encouraging the sharing of personal encounters. These interactions can lead to the discovery of previously unreported sightings or forgotten tales, enriching the narrative of the Loch Ness Monster. Additionally, community involvement fosters a sense of ownership and interest in preserving the cultural heritage of the region, further enhancing the tourism experience centered around the monster legend.

Lastly, the intersection of popular culture and the investigation of the Loch Ness Monster cannot be overlooked. Documentaries, television series, and artistic representations contribute to the ongoing fascination with the creature, often inspiring new waves of inquiry and exploration. These cultural products not only reflect the public's intrigue but also serve as platforms for disseminating findings from scientific investigations. By bridging the gap between folklore and empirical study, these methods of investigation ensure that the legend of the Loch Ness Monster remains vibrant and relevant, captivating the imaginations of cryptozoology enthusiasts and tourists alike.

## Famous Expeditions and Their Findings

Throughout history, numerous expeditions have sought to uncover the truth behind the enduring legend of the Loch Ness Monster. These quests, driven by a mix of curiosity and scientific inquiry, have contributed significantly to both the folklore surrounding Loch Ness and the broader field of cryptozoology. Each expedition has produced findings that not only invigorated public interest but also raised questions about the nature of the creature purported to inhabit these deep waters. From early investigations in the 1930s to modern scientific explorations, the stories of these expeditions have become an integral part of Loch Ness's rich tapestry of lore.

One of the most notable early expeditions occurred in 1934, when Dr. Robert Kenneth Wilson famously captured the "surgeon's photograph." This image, which purportedly depicted the creature's head and neck, ignited a media frenzy and solidified public fascination with the Loch Ness Monster. Although the photograph was later revealed to be a hoax, it served as a catalyst for further investigations and inspired subsequent expeditions. This initial foray into the depths of Loch Ness marked the beginning of a new era of exploration that combined folklore with a burgeoning interest in scientific methods.

In the decades that followed, several organized searches were conducted, including Operation Deepscan in 1987, which employed sonar technology to map the loch's depths. This extensive survey aimed to locate and identify any large creature that might inhabit the waters. While the operation did not yield definitive evidence of the Loch Ness Monster, it did discover numerous underwater structures and formations, suggesting that the loch is a complex ecosystem. Such findings have encouraged ongoing research into the environmental conditions of Loch Ness, prompting questions about how these factors might influence the legends surrounding its most famous resident.

The 2000s saw a resurgence of interest in Loch Ness with the advent of new technologies, including underwater drones and advanced imaging techniques. Expeditions during this period have focused on gathering empirical evidence to either support or debunk the existence of the monster. While some discoveries have been inconclusive, the efforts have led to a better understanding of the loch's unique biodiversity. These modern explorations serve as a testament to the enduring allure of the Loch Ness Monster, illustrating how technology can bridge the gap between folklore and scientific investigation.

The interplay between the findings of these expeditions and the local folklore surrounding Loch Ness has created a dynamic narrative that captivates tourists and cryptozoology enthusiasts alike. Each new expedition adds layers to the legend, encouraging both skepticism and belief. As visitors flock to the shores of Loch Ness, they become part of a living tradition that intertwines history, science, and myth. The tales of famous expeditions and their findings not only enrich the lore of the Loch Ness Monster but also highlight the profound impact this enigmatic creature has had on popular culture and the human psyche.

# 4

# The Loch Ness Monster in Popular Culture

## Literature and Folklore

Literature and folklore surrounding Loch Ness have woven a rich tapestry that captivates both locals and visitors, fueling the enduring legend of the Loch Ness Monster. This mythical creature, often described as a large aquatic being with a long neck and humps, has found a prominent place in Scottish folklore. The narratives surrounding Nessie—ranging from ancient tales of water beasts to modern sightings—reflect the deep cultural significance that the loch holds for the community. The interplay of myth and reality not only enriches the lore but also serves to attract tourists and cryptozoology enthusiasts alike, eager to explore the mysterious waters.

Historical accounts of Loch Ness Monster sightings date back centuries, with some of the earliest references appearing in Celtic folklore. The Picts, an ancient Scottish tribe, are said to have carved stone images of a creature resembling a serpent, hinting at long-standing beliefs in lake monsters. The legendary story of St. Columba in the 6th century, where he purportedly confronted a beast in the loch, further solidified Nessie's place in the annals of Scottish history. These early tales laid the groundwork for the modern phenomenon, demonstrating how folklore evolves while maintaining a connection to local heritage and identity.

As the Loch Ness Monster became a subject of scientific scrutiny in the 20th century, it also captured the imagination of popular culture. Literature, films, and television series have perpetuated the legend, often blending fact with fiction. Documentaries exploring the mystery of Nessie and dramatizations of famous sightings have reached audiences worldwide, further embedding the creature into global consciousness. This cultural fascination not only enhances tourism in the region but also encourages artistic interpretations, leading to a diverse range of representations from sculptures to paintings, each reflecting the artist's perspective on the elusive creature.

The search for Loch Ness and the scientific investigations into its depths have also been influenced by local folklore. Cryptozoologists have employed various methods, from sonar scanning to underwater photography, in hopes of uncovering evidence of Nessie's existence. Despite the lack of definitive proof, the blending of scientific inquiry with historical accounts and anecdotal tales continues to ignite debate within both the scientific community and the general public. This intersection of folklore and science illustrates the complexity of belief systems, as many individuals find themselves straddling the line between skepticism and fascination.

Ultimately, the literature and folklore surrounding Loch Ness contribute significantly to its allure as a destination. The stories of the Loch Ness Monster invite visitors to engage with the landscape in a unique way, fostering a sense of wonder and exploration. Local legends not only enhance the tourist experience but also encourage a deeper appreciation for the natural environment and its mysteries. As the legend of Nessie endures, it remains a testament to the power of storytelling, reflecting humanity's eternal quest to understand the unknown and the creatures that might inhabit it.

## Film and Television Representations

Film and television have played a significant role in shaping public perception of the Loch Ness Monster, transforming it from a local legend into a global phenomenon. Early cinematic representations, beginning in the mid-20th century, often focused on the mystery and allure of the Loch itself, setting the stage for countless fictional tales. These productions typically depicted the Loch Ness Monster as a fearsome creature lurking beneath the surface, tapping into deep-seated fears and fascination with the unknown. Such portrayals not only fueled interest in cryptozoology but also attracted tourists eager to experience the magic of Loch Ness firsthand.

Documentaries have contributed to the discourse surrounding Nessie, providing audiences with a blend of folklore, historical accounts, and scientific exploration. Shows like "The Loch Ness Monster: The Ultimate Guide" and various BBC documentaries have sought to debunk myths while also celebrating the enduring legend. By interviewing local witnesses, cryptozoologists, and scientists, these programs create a narrative that oscillates between skepticism and belief, inviting viewers to ponder the possibility of the monster's existence. This duality serves to enrich the legend while simultaneously fostering a deeper understanding of the cultural significance of such creatures in human history.

Television series have also found fertile ground in the mythology of Loch Ness, often incorporating the monster into broader themes of adventure and exploration. Shows like "Finding Bigfoot" and "Destination Truth" have ventured into the depths of the loch, presenting a blend of entertainment and investigation. These series not only entertain but also engage audiences in the ongoing quest for evidence, showcasing the lengths to which enthusiasts and skeptics alike will go to uncover the truth. The visual portrayal of the loch, coupled with dramatic storytelling, captivates viewers and sustains public interest in the legend.

Artistic interpretations in film and television have also reflected societal attitudes towards the Loch Ness Monster. Animated films and children's shows often present a more whimsical version of Nessie, appealing to younger audiences and contributing to a lighter, more fantastical view of the legend. In contrast, horror films may exaggerate the monster's ferocity, tapping into primal fears while amplifying the mystery surrounding the creature. These varying representations serve to highlight the diverse ways in which the Loch Ness Monster is perceived, reflecting broader cultural narratives and the changing nature of folklore.

The impact of these representations on tourism cannot be understated. The allure of the Loch Ness Monster has established a significant tourism industry in the region, with attractions ranging from boat tours to dedicated museums. Film and television have been instrumental in promoting Loch Ness as a destination for cryptozoology enthusiasts and curious travelers alike. As visitors flock to the loch, they bring with them a sense of wonder and inquiry that continues to invigorate local folklore. Ultimately, the interplay between film, television, and the legend of the Loch Ness Monster illustrates how cultural narratives evolve, shaping both belief and tourism in this iconic Scottish landscape.

## Merchandise and Commercialization

Merchandise and commercialization surrounding the Loch Ness Monster have evolved significantly over the years, transforming a local legend into a global phenomenon. From the early days of Loch Ness folklore, the creature captured the imaginations of local residents and visitors alike, inspiring a range of products that celebrate this enigmatic figure. Today, shops in nearby towns offer everything from plush toys and T-shirts emblazoned with Nessie's likeness to books, artwork, and even themed food items. This commercialization reflects not only the enduring allure of the Loch Ness Monster but also the local economy's dependence on tourism driven by this mythical creature.

Tourism is at the heart of the commercialization of Loch Ness, with thousands of visitors flocking to the area each year, drawn by the legend of Nessie. This influx has prompted local businesses to cater to cryptozoology enthusiasts and casual tourists alike. Guided boat tours on Loch Ness promise glimpses of the elusive monster, while informative exhibitions in local museums delve into historical accounts and scientific investigations. These experiences are often supplemented with merchandise that allows visitors to take a piece of the legend home, reinforcing their connection to the lore and enhancing the overall tourist experience.

Media representations of the Loch Ness Monster have also played a crucial role in merchandise development. Documentaries and television series exploring the mystery of Nessie have not only fueled public interest but have also inspired a plethora of related products. Collectibles, such as replica models of the monster and themed board games, have emerged as popular items among fans. Additionally, artistic interpretations found in local galleries and craft fairs serve as a testament to the cultural impact of the Loch Ness Monster, enriching the merchandise landscape with unique creations that celebrate this iconic figure.

The psychological aspect of belief in cryptids like the Loch Ness Monster contributes to the demand for related merchandise. For many, the thrill of the hunt for the unknown is as compelling as the creature itself. Products that allow individuals to engage with the lore—such as books detailing eyewitness accounts or guides to conducting their investigations—satisfy a curiosity that extends beyond mere tourism. This burgeoning market creates a symbiotic relationship between the legend and merchandise, as each fuels the other, reinforcing the narrative that surrounds Loch Ness.

Nonetheless, the commercialization of the Loch Ness Monster raises important considerations regarding the environmental impact on the region. Increased tourism can strain local ecosystems, particularly around the loch itself. Balancing the economic benefits of merchandise and tourism with the preservation of the natural landscape is crucial. Local authorities and businesses are increasingly aware of the need to promote sustainable practices, ensuring that the legend of Loch Ness can continue to captivate future generations without compromising the integrity of the environment that gives it life.

# 5

# Scientific Investigations and Evidence

## The Role of Technology in Research

Technology has profoundly transformed the landscape of research surrounding the Loch Ness Monster, enabling enthusiasts and scientists alike to explore this enigmatic creature more thoroughly than ever before. Advanced tools such as sonar imaging, underwater drones, and remote sensing have replaced the rudimentary methods of earlier investigations. These technologies allow researchers to penetrate the depths of Loch Ness with precision, mapping the lakebed and uncovering potential habitats for this elusive cryptid. The integration of digital technology has not only enhanced the quality of data collected but has also made it more accessible to the public, fostering a broader interest in the ongoing quest to uncover the truth behind the legends.

In addition to sonar and imaging technologies, the rise of citizen science has empowered amateur enthusiasts to participate in research efforts. Mobile apps and online platforms enable individuals to report sightings, share evidence, and collaborate on investigations. This democratization of data collection is significant in the context of the Loch Ness Monster, where anecdotal accounts and historical narratives have long shaped public perception. By leveraging technology, these contributions are systematically gathered and analyzed, providing a more comprehensive understanding of the patterns and credibility of sightings over the decades.

Social media and digital storytelling have also played a pivotal role in shaping the narrative surrounding Loch Ness. Platforms like Instagram, YouTube, and TikTok have become essential tools for sharing experiences, theories, and interpretations related to the Loch Ness Monster. The visual nature of these platforms brings the allure of the legend to a global audience, sparking interest in not only the creature itself but also the cultural and historical contexts that surround it. This widespread engagement often leads to increased tourism in the region, as people seek to connect with the folklore and participate in the stories they see online.

Scientific investigations into the Loch Ness Monster have been bolstered by advancements in genetic analysis, allowing researchers to test water samples for environmental DNA (eDNA). This innovative approach offers a unique method for detecting organisms that inhabit the lake without the need for direct observation. By analyzing eDNA, scientists can gather evidence about the biodiversity present in Loch Ness, potentially revealing whether a large, unknown species could exist. This method not only supports the search for the Loch Ness Monster but also contributes to the overall understanding of the lake's ecosystem and its environmental changes over time.

Ultimately, the role of technology in researching the Loch Ness Monster extends beyond mere data collection; it has redefined the relationship between folklore and science. As researchers and enthusiasts work together, fueled by technological advancements, the boundaries between myth and reality become increasingly blurred. This synergy fosters a deeper appreciation for not only the legend of the Loch Ness Monster but also the intricate tapestry of local culture, history, and environmental stewardship that defines the region. By embracing technology, the search for the Loch Ness Monster continues to evolve, captivating the imaginations of new generations while grounding the pursuit in scientific inquiry.

## Analysis of Photographic Evidence

The analysis of photographic evidence related to the Loch Ness Monster has been a cornerstone of both scientific inquiry and popular fascination. Over the decades, countless photographs have emerged, each claiming to capture a glimpse of this elusive creature. While some images have been unequivocally debunked as hoaxes or misidentified animals, others continue to spark debate among cryptozoology enthusiasts and skeptics alike. By examining the context, conditions, and content of these photographs, we can better understand their role in shaping public perception and belief in the Loch Ness Monster.

One of the most famous photographs is the so-called "Surgeon's Photograph," taken in 1934 by Colonel Robert Kenneth Wilson. This image purportedly shows a large creature surfacing in the loch. Although it was originally hailed as authentic, subsequent investigations revealed that it had been a staged photograph, using a toy submarine to simulate the monster. The evolution of this image from a symbol of the unknown to a representation of deception illustrates the challenges in discerning truth within the realm of cryptozoology. It also highlights how easily public perception can be swayed by compelling visual evidence, regardless of its authenticity.

Photographic evidence also encompasses a range of other images that have emerged over the years, including blurry shots and videos that claim to show the creature in action. Analyzing these visuals requires not only technical knowledge of photography but also an understanding of the psychological factors at play. Many viewers are predisposed to see what they want to believe, often interpreting indistinct shapes or shadows as evidence of the monster's existence. Such psychological phenomena underscore the complexities of belief in cryptids and the impact that compelling visuals can have on popular culture and folklore.

Scientific investigations into these photographs often involve image analysis techniques that can help determine authenticity. Various technologies, such as image enhancement and computer-generated imagery, provide tools for scrutinizing the details of these photos. Despite these advancements, the subjective nature of perception and belief complicates the interpretation of outcomes. Even when evidence appears to indicate a hoax or misidentification, the allure of the Loch Ness Monster persists, fueled by a deep-seated human desire for mystery and the unknown.

As we continue to explore the legends surrounding Loch Ness, the analysis of photographic evidence serves as a vital component of the broader narrative. It not only sheds light on the ongoing search for the Loch Ness Monster but also reflects the intricate interplay between folklore, scientific inquiry, and public imagination. Each photograph tells a story, contributing to the rich tapestry of legends that define Loch Ness, while also prompting us to consider our own beliefs and the nature of evidence in the pursuit of understanding the world around us.

## DNA Sampling and Environmental Studies

DNA sampling has emerged as a pivotal tool in the quest to unravel the mysteries surrounding the Loch Ness Monster. As cryptozoologists and researchers delve into the folklore and historical accounts of sightings, the application of modern scientific techniques offers a fresh perspective on these age-old legends. By collecting environmental DNA (eDNA) from the waters of Loch Ness, scientists can identify the presence of various species, both known and unknown, without the need for direct observation. This innovative method not only enhances our understanding of the ecosystem but also fuels the ongoing fascination with the possibility of undiscovered creatures lurking beneath the surface.

The methodology of eDNA sampling involves capturing genetic material shed by organisms into their environment. In the case of Loch Ness, researchers have conducted rigorous sampling across different locations and depths, seeking to catalog the biodiversity of this iconic body of water. The results can provide insights into the aquatic life that inhabits the loch, contributing to the broader discourse on the ecological health of the area. For tourists and enthusiasts captivated by the Loch Ness Monster legend, these scientific endeavors serve as a bridge between folklore and empirical investigation, igniting curiosity about what might truly reside within the depths.

As the search for the Loch Ness Monster continues, the intersection of science and local folklore becomes increasingly significant. Historical accounts of sightings often describe enormous, elusive creatures, which have inspired generations of explorers and adventurers. By employing DNA sampling techniques, researchers can evaluate whether these descriptions correlate with any known species or if they point to the existence of an unidentified creature. This scientific approach not only respects the rich tapestry of local legends but also seeks to validate or challenge them through evidence-based research, fostering a dialogue between myth and reality.

The implications of these studies extend beyond the Loch Ness Monster itself. Understanding the environmental impact on Loch Ness is crucial in preserving its unique ecosystem. With increasing tourism and the challenges posed by climate change, it is essential to monitor the health of the loch and the species that call it home. DNA sampling can reveal shifts in populations and biodiversity, allowing for informed conservation efforts. Such initiatives resonate with both locals and visitors who cherish the natural beauty and cultural significance of Loch Ness, ensuring that the legend endures for future generations.

Ultimately, the fusion of DNA sampling and environmental studies enriches the narrative of the Loch Ness Monster, appealing to cryptozoology enthusiasts and tourists alike. As scientific investigations continue to probe the depths of this legendary loch, they not only seek to uncover potential truths behind the monster but also to celebrate the cultural heritage that surrounds it. The ongoing exploration of Loch Ness serves as a reminder that the quest for knowledge often intertwines with the enchantment of folklore, creating a dynamic tapestry where science and legend coexist.

6

# Local Folklore and Legends Surrounding Loch Ness

## Ancient Myths and Stories

Ancient myths and stories surrounding Loch Ness have captivated the imaginations of locals and visitors alike for centuries. The loch itself, with its deep waters and mysterious depths, has been a fertile ground for folklore, spawning tales of creatures that dwell within its confines. From early Celtic legends to contemporary accounts, these narratives reflect humanity's enduring fascination with the unknown, serving as both cautionary tales and cultural touchstones that enrich the landscape of Scottish heritage.

One of the earliest references to a creature in Loch Ness can be traced back to the Life of St. Columba, a sixth-century text that recounts a miraculous encounter between the saint and a beast in the loch. According to the account, Columba intervened to save a man from the creature's grasp, demonstrating both the power of faith and the lingering dread of the unknown. This story not only highlights the spiritual significance of Loch Ness but also establishes a precedent for the monster's place in Scottish folklore, intertwining the narrative of the creature with the historical and religious identity of the region.

As the centuries progressed, the Loch Ness Monster evolved from a local legend into a symbol of intrigue that attracted attention beyond Scotland. The tales morphed into a tapestry of sightings and descriptions that varied widely, reflecting the cultural influences and storytelling traditions of the time. In the 19th century, reports of a large creature in the loch began to surface more frequently, coinciding with the rise of the Victorian fascination with the supernatural and the un-known. These accounts often included elaborate details, further embedding the monster into the collective consciousness and sparking a wave of interest that would lead to more modern explorations of the loch.

The impact of these ancient myths and stories extends into contemporary culture, influencing everything from literature and film to tourism and scientific inquiries. Cryptozoologists and enthusiasts continue to study and analyze the historical accounts, seeking evidence to support or debunk the existence of the Loch Ness Monster. This intersection of myth and science has created a unique niche within the broader field of cryptozoology, as researchers attempt to reconcile folklore with empirical investigation, all while keeping the spirit of the legends alive.

Ultimately, the myths and stories of Loch Ness serve not only to entertain but also to provoke deeper questions about belief, identity, and the relationship between humans and nature. The psychological allure of cryptids, particularly the Loch Ness Monster, taps into a fundamental curiosity about the mysterious aspects of our world. As tourists flock to Loch Ness in search of the creature, they become part of a living narrative that honors the ancient tales while contributing to the ongoing dialogue about what lies beneath the surface. This rich tapestry of folklore continues to inspire, reminding us that myths, whether rooted in truth or fiction, shape our understanding of the world around us.

## The Role of Local Communities

The local communities surrounding Loch Ness play a pivotal role in the ongoing fascination with the Loch Ness Monster, influencing both the folklore and the tourism that thrives in the region. These communities have lived alongside the loch for generations, weaving the legend of the monster into their cultural fabric. This deep-rooted connection contributes not only to the richness of the stories but also to the authenticity of the experiences offered to tourists and cryptozoology enthusiasts. Their narratives, passed down through oral tradition, shape the understanding and interpretation of the Loch Ness Monster, ensuring that the legend remains vibrant and relevant.

Local residents often serve as the first witnesses to alleged sightings and encounters with the creature, providing firsthand accounts that fuel curiosity and speculation. Many of these individuals have played a significant role in documenting their experiences, contributing to a growing archive of historical accounts that researchers rely on for evidence. This grassroots documentation fosters a sense of community ownership over the legend, as residents feel a personal connection to their shared history with the loch. Their contributions not only enrich the narrative but also invite tourists to engage with the local culture in a meaningful way.

Moreover, the economic impact of the Loch Ness Monster phenomenon cannot be understated. Local businesses, from bed-and-breakfast establishments to souvenir shops, thrive on the influx of visitors drawn by the allure of the monster. Community-led initiatives, such as guided tours and festivals celebrating Nessie, help sustain local economies while fostering a sense of pride among residents. By actively participating in the promo-

tion of the Loch Ness legend, locals create a symbiotic relationship with tourists, where both parties
benefit from the shared experience of exploring the
mystery of the loch.

The role of local communities extends beyond
economic benefits; they are also custodians of the
environment surrounding Loch Ness. Their inti-
mate knowledge of the landscape and its ecology
provides valuable insights into the environmental
impact of tourism and the need for sustainable
practices. As stewards of the loch, they advocate
for the preservation of the area's natural beauty,
ensuring that the lore of the Loch Ness Monster
is intertwined with a commitment to ecological responsibility. This perspective enriches the narrative
of the monster, framing it not just as a creature of
folklore, but as a symbol of the delicate balance between myth and nature.

Finally, the psychological aspect of belief in
cryptids like the Loch Ness Monster is often rein-
forced by the local community's enthusiasm. Their
acceptance and promotion of the legend create an
environment where belief can flourish, inviting
both skeptics and believers to explore the mysteries

of Loch Ness. This phenomenon fosters a unique cultural landscape where the lines between fact and fiction blur, allowing individuals to engage with the legend on various levels. In this way, the local communities not only preserve the lore but also provide a living context for understanding the enduring allure of the Loch Ness Monster in both local and global narratives.

## Modern Folklore and Its Evolution

Modern folklore surrounding the Loch Ness Monster has evolved significantly from its origins in the early accounts of a mysterious creature inhabiting the depths of the loch. Initially, tales of a water beast were passed down orally, with each generation adding its own details and embellishments. These stories often reflected the cultural beliefs and fears of the time, serving as cautionary tales or explanations for natural phenomena. As society transitioned into the modern era, the Loch Ness Monster became a symbol of intrigue and mystery, attracting attention from tourists, researchers, and cryptozoologists alike.

With the advent of technology and mass communication, the narrative surrounding the Loch Ness Monster began to shift. Photographs, videos, and documentaries proliferated, introducing new layers to the folklore. The infamous "Surgeon's Photo" of 1934, for example, catapulted the creature into the public consciousness, igniting widespread fascination and debate about its existence. This photograph, coupled with numerous sightings reported by locals and tourists, transformed the Loch Ness Monster from a regional legend into a global phenomenon, inspiring a multitude of interpretations that blended fact, fiction, and speculation.

As modern folklore continues to evolve, it incorporates elements from popular culture that further influence public perception of the Loch Ness Monster. Films, television series, and literature have all contributed to the mythos, often depicting the creature in fantastical ways. Such representations not only entertain but also shape the cultural narrative, reinforcing the allure of Loch Ness as a site of mystery. This interplay between folklore and popular culture demonstrates how legends can adapt to contemporary contexts while maintaining their core elements.

The scientific investigations into the Loch Ness Monster have also played a crucial role in shaping modern folklore. Researchers employing advanced sonar technology and environmental studies have sought to uncover the truth behind the monster's existence. While no definitive evidence has emerged, the ongoing search has fueled public interest and debate, allowing for a dynamic dialogue between believers and skeptics. This scientific approach has contributed to the folklore by adding a layer of legitimacy and complexity, inviting enthusiasts to engage with both the legend and the ongoing quest for answers.

In conclusion, modern folklore surrounding the Loch Ness Monster is a rich tapestry woven from historical accounts, popular culture, and scientific inquiry. As the legend continues to evolve, it reflects our collective fascination with the unknown and our desire to explore the boundaries of belief. For cryptozoology enthusiasts and Scotland tourists alike, the Loch Ness Monster serves not only as a captivating creature but also as a cultural phenomenon that invites exploration and inquiry into the very nature of myth and reality.

# 7

# Tourism and Loch Ness Monster Attractions

## Impact of Tourism on the Local Economy

The impact of tourism on the local economy surrounding Loch Ness is significant and multifaceted, particularly given the area's association with the legendary Loch Ness Monster. As tourists flock to this iconic location, they contribute to a vibrant economy that relies heavily on the influx of visitors drawn by both the mystery of the monster and the rich tapestry of local folklore. This economic boost manifests in various forms, from job creation in hospitality and retail sectors to increased demand for local attractions and services. Businesses ranging from quaint bed-and-breakfasts to guided tour operations thrive on the interest generated by the legend of the Loch Ness Monster, showcasing the profound relationship between folklore and economic viability.

The seasonal nature of tourism at Loch Ness also influences local employment patterns, with many residents engaging in seasonal work that aligns with peak visitor times. This fluctuation can present challenges, as local businesses must adapt to the ebb and flow of tourist numbers. However, it also encourages innovation in service offerings, prompting entrepreneurs to create year-round attractions that appeal to visitors interested in cryptozoology, history, and outdoor activities. As a result, the local economy experiences diversification, reducing dependency on any single industry and fostering resilience against economic downturns.

Moreover, the impact of tourism extends beyond immediate financial benefits; it fosters a sense of community identity tied to the Loch Ness Monster narrative. Residents often take pride in their association with the mythos, engaging in cultural initiatives that celebrate local legends through festivals, art, and educational programs. Such events not only enhance community cohesion but also attract even more tourists, perpetuating a cycle of economic growth. The legacy of the Loch Ness Monster thus becomes intertwined with the local culture, reinforcing the town's identity and creating a unique selling point that distinguishes it from other tourist destinations.

However, the economic benefits of tourism must be carefully balanced with environmental considerations. The increase in visitor numbers can lead to strain on local ecosystems, particularly around the loch itself. Issues such as littering, wildlife disturbance, and increased traffic can threaten the very landscapes that attract tourists. Local authorities and businesses are increasingly aware of the need for sustainable tourism practices that protect the natural beauty of Loch Ness while still allowing for economic growth. Initiatives aimed at educating tourists about responsible behavior and promoting conservation efforts are essential to ensure that the area's natural resources are preserved for future generations.

In conclusion, the interplay between tourism and the local economy at Loch Ness underscores the importance of folklore in driving economic activity. The legend of the Loch Ness Monster not only captivates the imaginations of tourists but also serves as a catalyst for local economic development. By fostering a sense of community and identity, encouraging sustainable practices, and supporting diverse business opportunities, the impact of tourism at Loch Ness illustrates how folklore can play a pivotal role in shaping both economic landscapes and cultural narratives. As interest in cryptozoology and the search for the Loch Ness Monster persists, so too does the potential for ongoing economic benefits for the region.

## Major Tourist Attractions and Sites

The Loch Ness area is home to a diverse array of tourist attractions that draw both cryptozoology enthusiasts and general visitors alike. The most iconic site is, of course, Loch Ness itself, a vast freshwater lake stretching approximately 23 miles in length and reaching depths of up to 755 feet. The loch is steeped in mystery and folklore, making it a focal point for those intrigued by the possibility of the legendary creature known as Nessie. Visitors often engage in boat tours that provide not only breathtaking views of the surrounding Highlands but also an opportunity to learn about the historical accounts of sightings and local legends that have captured the imaginations of many.

Another significant attraction is the Loch Ness Centre and Exhibition located in Drumnadrochit. This venue offers an immersive experience into the history and myth surrounding the Loch Ness Monster. The exhibition features interactive displays, historical footage, and detailed accounts of sightings that have occurred over the decades. It serves as a vital resource for those interested in the scientific investigations that have been conducted to uncover the truth behind the legend. The Centre also engages visitors through educational programs that delve into the environmental aspects of Loch Ness, promoting an understanding of how the ecosystem is closely linked to the lore of the monster.

For those seeking a more adventurous experience, the surrounding landscape offers numerous walking and cycling trails, such as the Great Glen Way, which runs alongside the loch. These trails not only provide stunning views of the water but also lead to various historical sites, such as Urquhart Castle. This medieval fortress, perched on the banks of Loch Ness, has its own share of legends and is a popular location for photography and exploration. The castle's rich history, combined with its association with the folklore of Nessie, makes it a must-visit site for anyone interested in the intricate tapestry of history and myth that characterizes the region.

The allure of Loch Ness extends into popular culture, with numerous films, documentaries, and television series dedicated to the mysterious creature. The annual Loch Ness Monster Festival celebrates this cultural phenomenon, featuring guest speakers, film screenings, and activities that engage both locals and tourists. This event not only highlights the ongoing fascination with Nessie but also fosters a sense of community among those who share an interest in cryptozoology. It underscores the significance of Loch Ness not just as a geographical landmark, but as a cultural icon that continues to influence art, literature, and media.

Finally, the psychological aspects of belief in cryptids like the Loch Ness Monster play a crucial role in the attraction of the site. Many visitors come seeking validation of their beliefs or simply to experience the thrill of the unknown. The phenomenon of Nessie taps into deeper human emotions and curiosities about the natural world and the mysteries it holds. As visitors explore the rich folklore and historical accounts, they engage in a collective experience that transcends mere tourism, becoming a part of the ongoing narrative that defines Loch Ness and its enigmatic inhabitant. This blend of natural beauty, historical intrigue, and cultural significance ensures that Loch Ness remains a vital destination for those drawn to the mystery of the monster and the legends surrounding it.

## The Balance Between Conservation and Tourism

The interplay between conservation and tourism at Loch Ness is a critical consideration for both the preservation of its unique ecosystem and the ongoing fascination with the legendary creature said to inhabit its depths. As one of Scotland's most iconic destinations, Loch Ness attracts millions of visitors annually, all eager to glimpse the elusive Nessie or to delve into the rich tapestry of folklore surrounding the loch. However, this influx of tourists poses significant challenges to the local environment, necessitating a careful balance that allows for both exploration and preservation.

In recent years, the local community and conservationists have recognized the importance of sustainable tourism practices. These practices aim to minimize the environmental footprint of visitors while still providing them with enriching experiences. Guided tours that emphasize ecological awareness and respect for the natural habitat are becoming increasingly popular. By educating tourists on the delicate balance of the loch's ecosystem, these initiatives foster a deeper appreciation for the area's natural beauty and the folklore that surrounds it.

Furthermore, the promotion of conservation efforts can enhance the tourism experience. Many visitors are not only interested in the tales of the Loch Ness Monster but are also drawn to the stunning landscapes and diverse wildlife that the area has to offer. By integrating conservation messages into tourism, local operators can create a narrative that highlights the interdependence of the loch's mythical allure and its environmental significance. This approach can lead to a more informed tourist base that values preservation as part of their visit.

Scientific investigations into the Loch Ness Monster have also played a role in this balance. Researchers often conduct studies that require access to the loch, leading to opportunities for tourists to participate in or observe these scientific endeavors. This interaction can demystify the search for Nessie while promoting a sense of stewardship toward the environment. When visitors understand the scientific methods used to explore their legends, they may become more invested in protecting the loch and its surroundings.

The ongoing dialogue between conservation and tourism at Loch Ness is essential for ensuring that both the legends of the past and the natural treasures of the present are preserved for future generations. As cryptozoology enthusiasts and tourists explore the depths of folklore and the possibility of undiscovered creatures, they must also embrace their role as custodians of this iconic site. By fostering a culture of respect and sustainability, Loch Ness can remain a vibrant testament to Scotland's rich heritage and natural beauty, continuing to captivate minds and hearts for years to come.

# 8

# Documentary Films and Television Series

## Notable Documentaries on Loch Ness

Documentary films have played a significant role in shaping the narrative around the Loch Ness Monster, blending historical accounts, scientific inquiry, and cultural fascination. Among the most notable is "The Loch Ness Monster: The Evidence," which meticulously examines the various sightings and claims surrounding the creature. Featuring interviews with eyewitnesses and cryptozoologists, the film delves into the murky depths of Loch Ness while presenting a balanced perspective on the evidence, or lack thereof, that has emerged over the decades. Its thorough analysis not only captivates viewers but also encourages critical thinking about the phenomena surrounding this legendary creature.

Another prominent documentary is "Nessie: The Truth," which takes a more skeptical approach. This film investigates the origins of the Loch Ness Monster legend, tracing it back to local folklore and societal influences that have perpetuated the myth over the years. By interviewing historians and scientists, the documentary seeks to debunk popular misconceptions, encouraging viewers to reconsider the validity of the numerous sightings reported throughout history. This critical perspective is crucial for cryptozoology enthusiasts who wish to understand the complexities behind such legends and the psychology of belief in cryptids.

"The Loch Ness Monster: A 50-Year Mystery" offers a unique blend of historical footage and modern scientific exploration. It chronicles significant milestones in the search for Nessie, including the infamous 1934 Surgeon's Photograph and subsequent investigations that have captured public imagination. The documentary highlights the technological advancements in sonar and underwater exploration that have allowed researchers to probe Loch Ness like never before. By showcasing both the excitement and the disappointments of these scientific endeavors, it provides a comprehensive overview of the ongoing quest for evidence of the elusive creature.

For those interested in the cultural impact of the Loch Ness Monster, "Legends of Loch Ness" serves as a fascinating exploration of how this myth has permeated popular culture. Featuring clips from films, television shows, and artistic representations, the documentary illustrates how Nessie has become a symbol of mystery and intrigue, inspiring countless creative interpretations. This cultural lens is essential for understanding the broader implications of the Loch Ness Monster legend, particularly for tourists drawn to the area seeking to engage with its rich tapestry of stories and attractions.

Lastly, "Nessie: The Environmental Impact" addresses the ecological considerations surrounding Loch Ness and how tourism tied to the monster affects the local environment. This documentary emphasizes the importance of preserving the natural beauty of the loch while catering to the curiosity of visitors. It highlights efforts by local communities and conservationists to maintain the delicate balance between promoting tourism and protecting the unique ecosystem of Loch Ness. Such discussions are vital for anyone keen on understanding the intersection of folklore, environmental stewardship, and the enduring allure of the Loch Ness Monster.

## The Influence of Television on Public Perception

Television has played a pivotal role in shaping public perception of the Loch Ness Monster, transforming an ancient legend into a modern phenomenon. From the early documentaries that presented purported evidence of the creature to sensationalized reality shows, the influence of this medium cannot be overstated. Each portrayal contributes to the collective consciousness surrounding the monster, often blurring the lines between folklore and reality. As viewers tune in, they are simultaneously entertained and educated, leading to a complex relationship with the mythos of Loch Ness.

The depiction of the Loch Ness Monster in television programming has varied widely, ranging from serious investigative documentaries to playful parodies. Early broadcasts, such as the BBC's "The Loch Ness Monster: The Truth," aimed to present a balanced view, weighing historical accounts against scientific skepticism. In contrast, more recent shows often prioritize sensationalism, emphasizing dramatic reenactments and bold claims without sufficient evidence. This shift has consequences for audiences, as sensationalized narratives can overshadow the rich tapestry of local folklore and the scientific inquiries that have been conducted over decades.

Television not only informs public perception but also stimulates tourism in the region. Many travelers are drawn to Loch Ness after experiencing its mythos through popular shows and documentaries. The portrayal of the monster as a mysterious and elusive creature fosters a sense of adventure, encouraging enthusiasts to embark on their own quests for evidence. Consequently, local businesses and attractions have capitalized on this interest, creating a symbiotic relationship between media representation and economic growth for the area.

Moreover, the psychological impact of these televised representations can influence belief systems surrounding cryptids. Audiences often find themselves emotionally invested in the search for the Loch Ness Monster, which can lead to a phenomenon known as "confirmation bias." This psychological tendency causes individuals to favor information that supports their existing beliefs while disregarding contradictory evidence. As television perpetuates narratives of encounters and sightings, it reinforces the notion that the Loch Ness Monster is more than just a myth, further entrenching it in popular culture.

In conclusion, the influence of television on public perception of the Loch Ness Monster is profound and multifaceted. It shapes not only how the creature is viewed and understood but also how it affects local culture and tourism. Through a blend of entertainment, education, and psychological engagement, television has woven the legend of the Loch Ness Monster into the fabric of contemporary society. As cryptozoology enthusiasts and tourists explore Loch Ness, they do so in a landscape heavily marked by the narratives crafted through screens, forever altering their experience of this iconic Scottish legend.

## Critiques of Media Representations

Critiques of media representations of the Loch Ness Monster often focus on the ways in which sensationalism and exaggeration can distort public perception and understanding of this enigmatic creature. The media has played a crucial role in shaping the narrative surrounding Loch Ness, frequently prioritizing entertainment value over factual accuracy. This tendency can lead to the oversimplification of complex folklore and scientific investigations, presenting the Loch Ness Monster primarily as a spectacle rather than a subject worthy of serious inquiry. Such representations can alienate those who seek a more nuanced understanding of the cultural and environmental significance of the loch and its storied past.

The portrayal of the Loch Ness Monster in popular culture is another aspect that merits critique. Countless films, books, and television series have contributed to the lore, often prioritizing dramatic embellishments. These interpretations can overshadow the rich historical accounts of sightings, transforming what might have been a legitimate mystery into a caricature of itself. The resulting depictions can perpetuate myths and misunderstandings, influencing public belief in cryptids and detracting from the serious study of Loch Ness and its ecology. This phenomenon raises important questions about the responsibilities of media creators in accurately representing folklore and the creatures that inhabit it.

Moreover, the influence of media representations extends to tourism in the Loch Ness area. Tour operators and local businesses often capitalize on the monster myth, creating attractions that cater to the sensationalized image of Nessie rather than the authentic cultural heritage of the region. While this commercialization can boost the local economy, it can also lead to environmental degradation as increased foot traffic and infrastructure development threaten the delicate ecosystem of Loch Ness. This tension between economic benefit and environmental preservation highlights the need for a balanced approach to both tourism and media portrayals.

Scientific investigations into the Loch Ness Monster have also been affected by media portrayals. While researchers aim to uncover the truth behind the legend through rigorous methodologies, sensationalized reports can undermine their efforts by creating unrealistic expectations among the public. When discoveries are framed in a way that aligns with popular narratives, it can obscure the genuine findings and foster a cycle of belief that is resistant to scientific inquiry. Critics argue that this disconnect hinders the advancement of cryptozoology as a legitimate field of study, reinforcing stereotypes that equate rigorous research with fanciful speculation.

Lastly, the psychology of belief in cryptids is intricately tied to how the media presents these creatures. The allure of the Loch Ness Monster is bolstered by a combination of folklore, personal narratives, and media sensationalism, leading to a complex interplay between belief and skepticism. As audiences consume these representations, they may become more inclined to accept fantastical elements as truth, blurring the line between reality and myth. This phenomenon underscores the importance of critical engagement with media narratives, encouraging both enthusiasts and skeptics to seek out authentic stories and scientific insights that honor the rich tapestry of Loch Ness's history and ecology.

# 9

# Artistic Interpretations and Representations

## Art Inspired by the Loch Ness Monster

Art inspired by the Loch Ness Monster is a unique blend of creativity and folklore, capturing the enduring fascination with this elusive creature. Artists from various disciplines have sought to interpret the legend, using their work to explore the mystery and allure that the Loch Ness Monster represents. From paintings and sculptures to photography and digital art, each piece reflects not only the creature's physical form but also the emotions and stories surrounding it. These artistic expressions are often rooted in historical accounts of sightings, drawing on the rich tapestry of narratives that have emerged over the decades.

One prominent theme in Loch Ness-inspired art is the juxtaposition of the serene Scottish landscape with the enigmatic presence of the monster. Many artists depict the loch itself, with its dark, deep waters serving as the perfect backdrop for the creature's shadowy silhouette. This interplay between nature and myth invites viewers to engage with their imaginations, encouraging them to ponder the possibility of what lies beneath the surface. These artworks often evoke a sense of wonder and curiosity, prompting discussions about the intersection of reality and folklore, and how our perceptions of the unknown shape our understanding of the world.

Sculptors have also embraced the Loch Ness Monster as a subject, creating pieces that celebrate its mythical status while exploring the themes of belief and skepticism. These three-dimensional representations can be found in various forms, from whimsical interpretations to more serious, realistic portrayals. Such sculptures serve not only as tourist attractions but also as conversation starters, encouraging visitors to reflect on the psychological aspects of belief in cryptids. The physicality of these works brings the creature to life, allowing audiences to engage with the legend in a tangible way, often sparking a desire to learn more about the ongoing quest for evidence of the monster's existence.

In the realm of popular culture, the Loch Ness Monster has inspired countless films, documentaries, and television series, further solidifying its status as a cultural icon. These productions often feature artistic depictions of the creature, ranging from fantastical animations to more serious dramatizations. The visual representation of the Loch Ness Monster in media plays a crucial role in shaping public perception, reinforcing the legend while also challenging viewers to consider the scientific investigations and evidence that accompany the folklore. This dynamic relationship between art and media continues to fuel interest in the monster, making it a central figure in discussions about cryptozoology and environmental impact on the loch.

The diverse artistic interpretations of the Loch Ness Monster reflect not only the creature's mythic status but also the broader cultural significance it holds for Scotland and beyond. Each piece of art contributes to the ongoing dialogue about the nature of belief, the allure of the unknown, and the importance of local folklore in shaping identity. As tourists flock to Loch Ness, drawn by the promise of encountering this legendary creature, the art inspired by the monster serves as a reminder of the power of stories to captivate and inspire. Through these creative expressions, the Loch Ness Monster remains an enduring symbol of mystery, inviting us to explore the depths of our imaginations and the natural world.

## The Role of Artists in Shaping the Legend

The influence of artists in shaping the legend of the Loch Ness Monster cannot be overstated. Throughout history, artists have played a pivotal role in visualizing and popularizing the mythos surrounding this enigmatic creature. Their interpretations have not only captured the imagination of the public but also contributed to the ongoing dialogue about its existence. Paintings, illustrations, and sculptures have served as both representations of the monster and reflections of societal beliefs and fears about the unknown. By translating folklore into visual art, these creators have helped solidify the Loch Ness Monster's place in cultural history.

Artists often draw inspiration from local legends, weaving narratives that resonate with the communal experience of those who share a connection to Loch Ness. Works by artists such as John Cobb and his evocative paintings of the loch have become iconic, fostering a sense of intrigue and mystery. These artistic representations invite viewers to engage with the lore, prompting questions about the nature of the creature and the historical accounts surrounding it. As tourists visit Loch Ness, they encounter these artistic interpretations, which enhance their experience and deepen their understanding of the local culture and its myths.

Moreover, the role of artists extends beyond mere representation; they also serve as ambassadors of the legend. Through their works, they communicate the rich tapestry of stories that have emerged over centuries, from ancient Celtic myths to contemporary sightings. This storytelling aspect is crucial, as it keeps the legend alive and relevant in modern discourse. Artists often collaborate with folklorists and historians, ensuring that their representations are grounded in the rich narrative tradition that surrounds Loch Ness. This collaboration further blurs the lines between fact and fiction, reinforcing the legend's allure.

The impact of artistic interpretation is also visible in the realm of tourism. As the Loch Ness Monster has become a symbol of Scottish identity, artists have created merchandise, souvenirs, and attractions that draw visitors from around the globe. These commercial endeavors not only celebrate the legend but also contribute to the local economy. The artwork serves as tangible reminders of the lore, allowing tourists to take a piece of the mystique home with them. This economic aspect highlights the symbiotic relationship between art, folklore, and tourism in the context of Loch Ness.

Finally, the ongoing debate surrounding the existence of the Loch Ness Monster is enriched by artistic contributions that provoke thought and discussion. Artists challenge audiences to confront their beliefs about cryptids and the nature of reality. By creating thought-provoking pieces that question the boundaries of belief and skepticism, they encourage viewers to explore not just the legend of the Loch Ness Monster but their own perceptions of the world. In this way, artists are not merely chroniclers of folklore; they are active participants in the ongoing dialogue about what it means to believe in the extraordinary.

## Contemporary Art and Loch Ness

Contemporary art has increasingly embraced the mystique and intrigue surrounding Loch Ness, weaving the legend of its elusive monster into various forms of artistic expression. Artists from diverse backgrounds have found inspiration in the folklore, historical accounts, and the enigmatic nature of the loch itself. This subchapter explores how contemporary artists engage with the legend of the Loch Ness Monster, creating pieces that reflect both the cultural significance of the myth and its impact on tourism and local identity.

Many artists utilize mixed media to capture the essence of Loch Ness and its legendary inhabitant. Installations and sculptures often draw upon the haunting beauty of the loch, juxtaposing natural elements with imaginative representations of the monster. For instance, some artists have created giant sculptures reminiscent of the creature, which not only serve as public art but also as attractors for tourists, fostering a dialogue between myth and reality. These works encourage locals and visitors alike to reflect on the narratives that shape their perceptions of the loch and its inhabitants.

In addition to physical artworks, contemporary digital art has emerged as a powerful medium for exploring the Loch Ness Monster mythos. Virtual reality experiences and interactive installations allow audiences to immerse themselves in the lore of the loch. Through these innovative approaches, artists can simulate sightings, allowing participants to engage with the legend in a uniquely personal way. This blend of technology and mythology not only enhances the allure of Loch Ness but also highlights how contemporary art can serve as a vessel for storytelling and community engagement.

Artistic interpretations of the Loch Ness Monster also play a significant role in popular culture, influencing how the legend is perceived and perpetuated. From illustrations in children's books to featured segments in documentaries, these representations shape the collective imagination surrounding the creature. Artists often take liberties with the depiction of the monster, reflecting broader themes such as the relationship between humanity and nature, the unknown, and the psychological allure of cryptids. This multifaceted portrayal fosters a deeper understanding of why Loch Ness continues to captivate the public's imagination.

Ultimately, the intersection of contemporary art and the Loch Ness legend illustrates the enduring power of folklore in shaping cultural identity and tourism. As artists reinterpret and reimagine the monster, they contribute to a dynamic dialogue that keeps the legend alive in the modern era.

For cryptozoology enthusiasts and tourists alike, these artistic expressions enhance the experience of Loch Ness, inviting exploration and contemplation of its mysteries while celebrating the rich tapestry of local folklore that has endured for generations.

# 10

# Environmental Impact on Loch Ness

## Ecological Studies of Loch Ness

Ecological studies of Loch Ness provide vital insights into the biodiversity and environmental conditions of this iconic Scottish lake, which has long been associated with legends of the Loch Ness Monster. The unique ecosystem of Loch Ness, characterized by its deep waters and rich nutrient levels, supports a variety of aquatic life, including fish species such as salmon and trout. These ecological factors contribute to the intriguing atmosphere that fuels the ongoing interest in both the natural environment and the myths surrounding the elusive creature. Over the years, researchers have aimed to understand how this ecosystem functions and how it may have influenced historical accounts of sightings and the folklore that has emerged from the area.

One significant aspect of ecological studies is the focus on water quality and its impact on the flora and fauna within Loch Ness. The lake's deep, murky waters create a unique habitat, but they also pose challenges for researchers. Regular monitoring of water temperature, nutrient levels, and pollution is essential for maintaining the health of the ecosystem. As the lake attracts numerous tourists and cryptozoology enthusiasts, understanding these environmental dynamics becomes even more crucial. Healthy aquatic ecosystems not only support local wildlife but also ensure that the myths and legends surrounding Loch Ness continue to thrive in a world increasingly impacted by human activity.

In addition to examining the biological aspects of Loch Ness, researchers delve into the historical accounts of monster sightings that may be influenced by ecological factors. For instance, the presence of large fish or unusual underwater formations could lead to misinterpretations of what witnesses perceive as a mysterious creature. As cryptozoologists analyze these encounters, they often consider how environmental conditions might affect visibility and the behavior of aquatic life, thereby contributing to the lore of the Loch Ness Monster. The interplay between ecology and folklore underscores the importance of scientific investigation in discerning fact from fantasy.

Moreover, the environmental impact of tourism on Loch Ness cannot be overlooked. The influx of visitors drawn to the lake in search of the monster has led to increased scrutiny of how such activities affect the fragile ecosystem. Studies indicate that certain tourist practices may disrupt local wildlife and contribute to water pollution. Consequently, ecologists advocate for sustainable tourism practices that balance the desire for exploration and adventure with the need to preserve the natural beauty and ecological integrity of Loch Ness. Educational initiatives aimed at tourists can enhance awareness of environmental responsibility while enriching their experience of the lake's lore.

As the study of Loch Ness continues to evolve, the intersection of ecology and folklore remains a captivating area of exploration for both scientists and enthusiasts. The ongoing search for the Loch Ness Monster serves as a compelling lens through which to examine broader ecological concepts and their cultural implications. By understanding the ecological dynamics of Loch Ness, cryptozoology enthusiasts and tourists alike can appreciate the lake not only as a site of legend but also as a vital ecosystem that deserves protection and respect. This dual perspective enriches the narrative of Loch Ness, allowing for a deeper connection to both its natural environment and the captivating stories that have emerged from its depths.

## Human Impact on the Ecosystem

Human activities have significantly shaped the ecosystem of Loch Ness, influencing not only its physical landscape but also the folklore and cultural narratives surrounding it. The Loch, famed for its mysterious inhabitant, the Loch Ness Monster, has been subject to various human interventions over the years. From industrial developments to tourism, each action has left its mark, altering the delicate balance of the region's natural environment. Understanding these impacts is crucial for cryptozoology enthusiasts and tourists alike, as they explore the rich tapestry of myths and realities associated with Loch Ness.

One of the most notable human impacts on the Loch is the introduction of various pollutants and waste products. Over the decades, industrial activities, particularly from nearby towns, have contributed to water contamination. This pollution not only threatens the aquatic life within Loch Ness but also raises questions about the health of any creatures that might inhabit its depths. Cryptozoologists often emphasize the importance of clean ecosystems when searching for elusive species, suggesting that the degradation of the Loch could obscure signs of the Loch Ness Monster and other wildlife.

Tourism has also played a pivotal role in shaping the Loch's environment. With millions of visitors flocking to the site each year to catch a glimpse of its legendary monster, the pressure on local resources has increased. Infrastructure developments, such as hotels, restaurants, and visitor centers, have transformed the landscape, often at the expense of natural habitats. While tourism provides economic benefits and keeps the lore of the Loch alive, it simultaneously poses challenges to the preservation of the natural environment, necessitating a balance between visitor engagement and ecological conservation.

Furthermore, the rise of popular culture surrounding the Loch Ness Monster has led to an increase in recreational activities, including boating and fishing. While these pursuits can enhance the visitor experience, they may also disturb the local wildlife and disrupt the natural order of the ecosystem. Cryptozoologists argue that understanding these dynamics is essential for both the preservation of the Loch's unique environment and the ongoing search for cryptids. By fostering responsible tourism and recreation, enthusiasts can help safeguard the Loch and its legendary inhabitants.

In conclusion, the human impact on the Loch Ness ecosystem is a multifaceted issue that intertwines with the lore and legend of the Loch Ness Monster. For those captivated by the stories and the search for this enigmatic creature, recognizing the environmental challenges posed by human activity is vital. As custodians of this legendary site, both locals and visitors must advocate for sustainable practices that honor the rich history, culture, and ecology of Loch Ness, ensuring that future generations can continue to marvel at its mysteries.

## Conservation Efforts and Future Challenges

Conservation efforts surrounding Loch Ness have become increasingly vital as the intersection of environmental sustainability and tourism continues to evolve. The loch, renowned for its legendary inhabitant, the Loch Ness Monster, attracts millions of visitors each year. This influx places considerable pressure on the delicate ecosystem of the loch. Local authorities and conservation groups have initiated various programs to safeguard the natural environment while still promoting the mythos of the creature that has captivated countless generations. These efforts aim to balance ecological preservation with the economic benefits derived from tourism, ensuring that both the folklore and the natural beauty of Loch Ness can endure.

One of the primary initiatives has been the promotion of sustainable tourism practices. This includes encouraging visitors to adhere to guidelines that minimize their environmental footprint, such as responsible waste disposal and maintaining designated paths to prevent erosion. Additionally, educational programs have been developed to inform tourists about the unique biodiversity of Loch Ness and the importance of preserving its habitats. By fostering a sense of stewardship among visitors, these programs aim to cultivate respect for both the folklore and the natural environment of this iconic location.

Despite these efforts, future challenges loom on the horizon. Climate change poses a significant threat to the ecological integrity of Loch Ness, potentially altering water levels and affecting species that have thrived in the loch for centuries. Additionally, increased boat traffic and potential pollution from local industries can disrupt the fragile ecosystem. As the demand for cryptozoological tourism grows, it is crucial that stakeholders actively engage in monitoring and mitigating these environmental impacts while still celebrating the rich tapestry of legends that surround the loch.

Scientific investigations into the Loch Ness Monster have contributed to both a fascination with the creature and an understanding of its natural habitat. Researchers employ modern technologies, such as sonar mapping and environmental DNA analysis, to explore the loch's depths. These scientific endeavors not only seek to uncover the truth behind the legendary monster but also serve as a means of gathering data essential for conservation efforts. The findings can provide insights into the health of the loch, guiding future protective measures and ensuring that the lore surrounding the monster does not overshadow the necessity of environmental preservation.

As the legend of the Loch Ness Monster continues to be interwoven with local folklore and popular culture, it is essential to recognize the role of these narratives in shaping public perception and action regarding conservation. The stories of the monster serve as a powerful reminder of the interconnectedness of myth and nature, underscoring the importance of preserving both the ecological and cultural heritage of Loch Ness. By fostering a deeper understanding of this relationship, enthusiasts, tourists, and conservationists can collectively ensure that the enchanting tales and the natural wonders of Loch Ness endure for generations to come.

# 11

# The Psychology of Belief in Cryptids

## Understanding Cryptozoological Beliefs

Cryptozoological beliefs encompass a fascinating intersection of folklore, personal testimony, and scientific inquiry, particularly when examining the Loch Ness Monster. These beliefs often stem from centuries of local lore, where stories of mysterious creatures lurking in the depths of Loch Ness have been passed down through generations. Enthusiasts are drawn to these narratives, intrigued by the possibility that such a creature might exist, despite the lack of definitive evidence. This allure is enhanced by the dramatic landscape of the Scottish Highlands, which serves as a backdrop for both the legends and the ongoing quest for truth.

Historical accounts of Loch Ness Monster sightings have played a pivotal role in shaping public perception of cryptozoology. From the first recorded sighting in the sixth century to the infamous photographs of the 20th century, each narrative contributes to a tapestry of intrigue. These stories often reflect deeper cultural themes, such as humanity's relationship with nature and the unknown. As tourists flock to Loch Ness, they not only seek the thrill of spotting the monster but also engage with the rich history that surrounds it, encountering a blend of fact and fiction that captivates their imaginations.

The search for the Loch Ness Monster has inspired numerous scientific investigations, which often seek to debunk myths while also fostering a spirit of curiosity. Researchers employ advanced technology like sonar and underwater cameras, hoping to provide concrete evidence of the creature's existence. However, many cryptozoology enthusiasts argue that the essence of the Loch Ness Monster transcends mere scientific validation. For them, the monster symbolizes the mysteries that lie beyond the grasp of modern science, representing a realm where belief and skepticism coexist, fueling ongoing debates about evidence and interpretation.

Popular culture has further entrenched the Loch Ness Monster within the global consciousness, as it has been featured in films, literature, and various media formats. These representations not only entertain but also contribute to the mystique surrounding the creature. By examining these portrayals, enthusiasts can gain insight into societal attitudes toward cryptids and the ways in which these legends are adapted over time. The Loch Ness Monster serves as a cultural icon, embodying both a sense of wonder and the human desire to explore the unknown.

Understanding the psychology of belief in cryptids sheds light on why the Loch Ness Monster continues to capture the hearts and minds of many. The phenomenon of belief in creatures like Nessie often stems from a combination of personal experiences, cultural narratives, and a desire for connection with the natural world. In an age where scientific explanations dominate, the allure of the unexplained remains powerful. Cryptozoological beliefs serve not only as a form of entertainment but also as a means for individuals to engage with the world around them, fostering a sense of belonging within a community that shares a passion for the extraordinary.

## The Role of Fear and Fascination

Fear and fascination are two powerful emotions that have shaped the narrative surrounding the Loch Ness Monster, deeply influencing both local folklore and the broader cultural perception of this enigmatic creature. For centuries, tales of a monstrous inhabitant lurking beneath the surface of Loch Ness have captivated the imaginations of locals and tourists alike. This duality of emotion not only fuels the legend but also serves as a magnet for those drawn to the mystery of the loch. The fear of the unknown, combined with a fascination for the extraordinary, creates a compelling tapestry that keeps the legend alive and thriving.

Historical accounts of Loch Ness Monster sightings reveal how fear often intertwines with fascination. Many early reports describe encounters that instilled genuine terror in witnesses, with descriptions of a massive, serpentine creature rising from the depths. Yet, these frightening experiences are often juxtaposed with an intense desire to understand and connect with the unknown. This paradox is reflected in the various responses from those who claim to have seen the creature; while some express dread, others are inspired to embark on personal quests to uncover the truth behind the legend. This ongoing interplay between fear and fascination ensures that the lore surrounding Loch Ness remains dynamic and ever-evolving.

The field of cryptozoology, dedicated to the study of creatures whose existence is not substantiated by mainstream science, thrives on this duality. Enthusiasts are often motivated by a blend of skepticism and belief, fueled by the fear of being misled or the thrill of discovering something extraordinary. As researchers sift through historical accounts, analyze photographic evidence, and conduct underwater explorations, they experience the tension of wanting to confront their fears while simultaneously nurturing their fascination for the Loch Ness Monster. This pursuit is not just about proving or disproving the creature's existence; it is about engaging with the emotions that the legend evokes.

In popular culture, the Loch Ness Monster serves as a symbol of both fear and fascination, appearing in literature, films, and art that explore the depths of human imagination. The creature's portrayal often reflects societal anxieties while simultaneously inviting audiences to marvel at the possibility of the extraordinary. Documentaries and television series frequently highlight this theme, presenting the monster as both a source of dread and a captivating subject of study. As tourists flock to Loch Ness, they bring with them a complex blend of emotions—curiosity, excitement, and trepidation—that enriches the cultural landscape surrounding the area.

The psychological aspects of belief in cryptids, particularly in the case of the Loch Ness Monster, illustrate how fear and fascination can coexist and motivate individuals. The psychological thrill of confronting one's fears while engaging with the fantastical can be a compelling draw. For many, the Loch Ness experience transcends the mere possibility of encountering a creature; it becomes an exploration of their own beliefs, fears, and desires. As the legend continues to evolve, it serves as a reminder of the power of folklore to capture the human spirit, revealing how fear and fascination can together create a timeless narrative that resonates across generations.

## Case Studies of Believers and Skeptics

The Loch Ness Monster, often affectionately referred to as "Nessie," has captivated both believers and skeptics for decades, creating a rich tapestry of stories and debates that highlight the intersection of folklore, personal experience, and scientific inquiry. Among the most compelling case studies are those that illustrate the deep emotional and psychological connections individuals have with the legend of Nessie. For believers, the monster represents hope, mystery, and a profound connection to the natural world. Skeptics, on the other hand, often approach the phenomenon with a critical eye, seeking rational explanations for sightings and the allure of the legend. This dichotomy not only fuels ongoing discussions but also enriches the cultural narrative surrounding Loch Ness.

One of the most notable believer case studies is that of Alastair D. McNab, a local fisherman who claimed to have had a close encounter with Nessie in 1975. McNab described an enormous creature surfacing near his boat, which he characterized as a long, serpentine animal. His testimony was not merely a fleeting experience but a life-altering moment that deepened his attachment to the Loch and its mysteries. This encounter prompted him to conduct his own informal investigations, gathering stories from other locals and tourists. His passionate advocacy for Nessie's existence highlights how personal experiences can transcend mere belief, intertwining with identity and community.

On the skeptic side, Dr. Neil Gemmell, a New Zealand geneticist, epitomizes the scientific approach to the Loch Ness phenomenon. In 2018, Gemmell led a team that collected and analyzed water samples from Loch Ness to search for environmental DNA (eDNA) that could indicate the presence of previously unrecognized species. His findings did not reveal any evidence of a large, undiscovered creature, but rather a diverse ecosystem of known species. Gemmell's work illustrates the rigorous scientific methodology that skeptics employ to demystify the legend, emphasizing the importance of empirical evidence in understanding natural phenomena. His approach serves as a reminder that skepticism and belief can coexist, each providing valuable insights into the mysteries of Loch Ness.

The cultural impact of the Loch Ness Monster has also been shaped by artistic interpretations and representations that resonate with both believers and skeptics. Artists, filmmakers, and writers have utilized the legend to explore themes of fear, wonder, and the unknown, often blurring the lines between reality and fiction. Documentaries and television series have played a significant role in popularizing Nessie, offering a platform for both sides to present their arguments. These media portrayals influence public perception, with believers finding validation in sensationalized accounts and skeptics highlighting the need for critical examination of the evidence presented.

Ultimately, the case studies of believers like Mc-Nab and skeptics like Gemmell reveal the complex relationship between folklore, personal belief, and scientific inquiry. The ongoing fascination with the Loch Ness Monster serves as a microcosm for broader discussions about the nature of belief in cryptids and the human desire to explain the inexplicable. Whether one approaches Nessie with an open heart or a critical mind, the legend continues to inspire exploration and dialogue, making Loch Ness a unique destination for both cryptozoology enthusiasts and tourists seeking to connect with the lore of Scotland. Through these narratives, the Loch Ness Monster remains a symbol of the enduring allure of mystery, inviting all to partake in its rich history.

# 12

# Conclusion and Future of Loch Ness Mysteries

## Continuing the Search for the Loch Ness Monster

The search for the Loch Ness Monster remains an enduring endeavor that captivates both enthusiasts of cryptozoology and the countless tourists drawn to the Scottish Highlands. Despite centuries of myths and reports of sightings, the elusive creature continues to be a subject of fascination and speculation. As technology advances, new methods for investigating the depths of Loch Ness have emerged, allowing researchers to explore areas previously deemed inaccessible. From sonar mapping to underwater drones, these innovative tools provide a clearer picture of the loch's ecosystem and the possibility of undiscovered species, while also fueling the legend of Nessie.

Historical accounts of Loch Ness Monster sightings date back to the sixth century, with the most famous being St. Columba's encounter with a mysterious creature. Over the years, reports of unusual phenomena and strange sightings have accumulated, contributing to a rich tapestry of folklore surrounding the loch. Each story, whether credible or fanciful, adds depth to the legend, intertwining the past with the present. These historical narratives not only fascinate visitors but also serve as a reminder of the cultural significance of the Loch Ness Monster within Scottish heritage.

In the realm of scientific investigations, numerous studies have attempted to validate the existence of the Loch Ness Monster. Researchers have employed various methodologies, including environmental DNA (eDNA) sampling, which analyzes genetic material in the water. Such studies have provided insights into the biodiversity of Loch Ness, revealing the presence of known species while also leaving room for speculation about what may lie beneath the surface. The balance between scientific inquiry and the enchanting allure of the monster creates a unique dynamic, as researchers navigate the intersection of evidence and belief.

The Loch Ness Monster has also permeated popular culture, inspiring films, literature, and art that further enhance its mystique. From documentaries exploring the phenomenon to fictional representations in movies, Nessie has become a symbol of intrigue and wonder. These portrayals not only entertain but also contribute to the ongoing dialogue about the creature's existence, shaping public perception and encouraging a sense of adventure among tourists. Such cultural artifacts serve as both a testament to the impact of the legend and a reflection of society's enduring fascination with the unknown.

As the search for the Loch Ness Monster continues, it is essential to consider the environmental implications of this pursuit. Increased tourism can strain local ecosystems, prompting discussions about the balance between exploration and conservation. Understanding the psychology of belief in cryptids like Nessie also plays a crucial role in this narrative. The desire to believe in something extraordinary can drive individuals to seek out experiences that connect them with the past and the possibility of the unknown. Ultimately, the quest for the Loch Ness Monster is as much about the journey itself as it is about discovering the truth behind one of Scotland's most enduring legends.

## Implications for Cryptozoology

The implications for cryptozoology in the context of Loch Ness extend far beyond the mere existence of the creature often referred to as Nessie. This legendary being has inspired a plethora of scientific inquiries and has become a focal point for those interested in the study of cryptids. The ongoing fascination with the Loch Ness Monster exemplifies the intersection between folklore, popular culture, and scientific investigation. Each sighting, whether genuine or fabricated, contributes to a larger narrative that fuels both skepticism and belief, ultimately shaping the public's perception of cryptozoology as a legitimate field of study.

Historical accounts of Loch Ness Monster sightings provide a rich tapestry of narratives that cryptozoologists can analyze. From ancient texts to modern-day testimonies, these accounts reveal the evolving nature of the creature's portrayal. Early descriptions often emphasized the monster's serpent-like features, while contemporary sightings have diversified the imagery, suggesting a variety of interpretations influenced by cultural and technological changes. Studying these accounts allows cryptozoologists to understand not only the legends themselves but also the psychological and sociological factors that drive belief in such creatures.

The search for the Loch Ness Monster has spurred numerous scientific investigations, ranging from sonar explorations to environmental studies of the loch's ecosystem. These efforts highlight the balance that must be struck between genuine scientific inquiry and the sensationalism often associated with the legend. While many studies have failed to provide concrete evidence of Nessie's existence, the methodologies employed contribute to a greater understanding of the loch's biodiversity and hydrology. Such investigations offer valuable insights that transcend mere cryptozoological interest and touch upon broader ecological concerns.

Local folklore and legends surrounding Loch Ness enhance the region's cultural identity and tourism appeal. The monster has become an integral part of the Scottish heritage, influencing everything from local festivals to souvenir shops. This cultural significance underscores the role of cryptozoology not only as a pursuit of the unknown but also as a means of preserving and celebrating local traditions. For tourists, the allure of the Loch Ness Monster serves as a gateway into Scotland's rich folklore, prompting deeper explorations of the region's history and natural beauty.

Finally, the portrayal of the Loch Ness Monster in popular culture, including documentary films and artistic interpretations, continuously shapes public perception and belief. These representations often blur the lines between fact and fiction, reinforcing the mythos surrounding Nessie. As cryptozoologists navigate this complex landscape, they must contend with the psychological aspects of belief in cryptids, recognizing that the desire to believe in the Loch Ness Monster is as significant as any empirical evidence that may or may not exist. The implications for cryptozoology, therefore, extend into realms of culture, psychology, and environmental awareness, creating a multifaceted field ripe for exploration and understanding.

## The Enduring Legacy of Loch Ness

The legacy of Loch Ness extends far beyond the captivating tales of its elusive monster. The intertwining of history, folklore, and contemporary culture has created a rich tapestry that continues to draw interest from cryptozoology enthusiasts and tourists alike. The legend of the Loch Ness Monster, often affectionately referred to as "Nessie," has become a symbol not just of Scotland's scenic landscapes but also of the human desire to explore the unknown. This enduring legacy serves as a testament to the profound impact of folklore on local identity and tourism, shaping perceptions of Loch Ness for generations.

Historical accounts of Loch Ness monster sightings date back to ancient times, with references found in both Pictish stones and Celtic legends. These narratives have evolved, adapting to the cultural context of their times, yet they consistently reflect a deep-seated fascination with the lake. Each reported sighting, whether it be the infamous photograph of 1934 or the more recent testimonies, adds layers to the legend, sparking debates among skeptics and believers alike. Such historical accounts not only contribute to the lore but also enhance the mystique of Loch Ness, making it a focal point for those interested in the intersection of history and cryptozoology.

The search for the Loch Ness Monster has galvanized scientific inquiry and public interest alike. Various expeditions have employed advanced technologies, from sonar mapping to underwater drones, in an effort to uncover evidence of Nessie. Although definitive proof remains elusive, these scientific investigations have yielded valuable insights into the ecology of Loch Ness, highlighting its unique environment and biodiversity. The ongoing quest for the monster has thus fostered a greater appreciation for the lake itself, transforming the search into an exploration of both myth and reality.

Nessie's presence in popular culture further solidifies her status within the global imagination. From films and television series to merchandise and local attractions, the Loch Ness Monster has permeated various forms of media. These representations not only contribute to the mythos surrounding Loch Ness but also stimulate tourism, bringing visitors eager to experience the allure of the legend. The way Nessie has been depicted in artistic interpretations—from whimsical illustrations to serious documentaries—reflects society's changing attitudes towards folklore and the natural world, illustrating how legend can inspire creativity.

Finally, the psychological dimensions of belief in cryptids like the Loch Ness Monster cannot be overlooked. The enduring allure of Nessie speaks to a fundamental aspect of human nature: the quest for meaning in the unexplained. The belief in such creatures often transcends mere curiosity, tapping into deeper themes of hope, wonder, and the search for connection with the natural world. As tourists and enthusiasts gather around the loch, they engage not only with the legend itself but also with the psychological narratives that shape their experiences. This legacy, rooted in folklore, scientific inquiry, and cultural expression, continues to thrive, ensuring that Loch Ness remains a captivating destination for those intrigued by the mysteries that lie beneath its waters.